A few years ago, *The Washington Post* conducted an experiment.

It involved the world-renowned, Grammy Award-winning violinist, Joshua Bell. Bell had entranced audiences in concert halls all over the world. People paid hundreds of dollars to watch him play on his $3.5 million Stradivarius violin. He's a virtuoso in his field and a total genius.

Yet one January morning, *The Washington Post* invited Mr Bell to exchange his white tie and tails for blue jeans and a baseball cap, swap the bright lights of the stage for a dirty Washington DC subway station, and busk some of music's most notoriously difficult pieces right there at the entrance.

The Washington Post called it "a test of people's perceptions and priorities". Would people perceive the presence of greatness? Would they prioritise stopping to listen?

Short answers: no and no.

You can watch the video on YouTube. Over the course of 40 minutes, amid the hundreds of people passing by, just seven paused to listen, and only one person recognised him. Three days previously Bell had played the same pieces at a sell-out concert at Boston's Symphony Hall, where people had paid as much as $100 a ticket. That morning outside the metro, he collected just $32.

Joshua Bell reflected on the experience afterward: "It was a strange feeling that people were ignoring me."

So how did hundreds of people walk past the presence of greatness without even realising it? Probably because, if you've done the same journey on public transport every day for years, you don't expect a world-class musician to entertain you at the station. You expect the guy with the violin to be just another busker, or you zone out the sound altogether. And so you walk on by, totally oblivious to what you're missing out on.

Can you imagine how you'd feel if you got home and saw on the news that someone famous had been where you were that day? What if you even saw yourself walking by on the footage?

I love the story about Joshua Bell because it reminds us that when we're not expecting something, we can often miss it. There's a saying that "familiarity breeds contempt"—or at the very least, complacency. The familiarity of a situation, or of a place, or of a time, can cause you to disregard the thing in front of you because you can't see that it's valuable. You just walk by on autopilot. We do it all the time (but of course, we don't even realise it).

It's possible for something similar to happen with Christmas.

After all, we've travelled along these festive paths so often, year after year. It's just another Christmas. We know what to expect: the lights, the sparkles, the ads, the decorations, the feasting, the presents, the tree, the traditions, the Christmas parties, the Christmas movies, with the music of Mariah Carey and Michael Bublé playing on loop in every shop from here to the North Pole...

All that stuff is great (well, almost all of it—you might be more of a "Joshua Bell" than a "Mariah Carey" kind of person). But like a commuter who is determined to catch their train, if we're powering towards 25th December it's possible to be so dulled by those familiar things that we walk past the main act in Christmas: Jesus.

We "zone out" to the "Christ" bit of Christmas, who often gets left behind in all the wrapping paper and the trimmings. But if we do that, we miss out on something incredible right in front of us. Here's what the Bible says was happening at that first Christmas. This isn't "just another" anything:

> *"The Word became flesh and made his dwelling among us. We have seen his glory, the glory of the one and only Son, who came from the Father, full of grace and truth."*
>
> *(The Gospel of John, chapter 1, verse 14)*

In those two short sentences the writer, John, makes three massive claims that get to the heart of Christmas. Don't rush past them—stop, listen and enjoy the music.

1. GOD CAME IN SKIN

"The Word became flesh and made his dwelling among us."

Most of us assume that religion is about trying to hunt God out, like some kind of adventure film: *The Raiders of the Lost God.* Or like children playing hide and seek:

Say your prayers—getting warmer.

Go to Christmas candlelight service—getting warmer.

Go to church any other time of year—getting warmer.

Go on a pilgrimage—getting *really* warm.

But if we're playing hide and seek with God, it's not God doing the hiding, but us. This verse is telling us that God's not hiding. Rather than keeping himself at arms length from society, withdrawn in his divine glory, God—described here by the intriguing title "the Word"—became one of us: "The Word became flesh". In the person of Jesus, God came to earth at Christmas and said, "I'm here".

One old carol puts it like this: "He came down to earth from heaven". The eternal creator God squeezed himself down into a 7 lb 8 oz(ish) baby.

Or in the words of another carol, when people looked at Jesus they could "veiled in flesh the godhead see". Can you imagine that? Cradling in your arms this little baby—God himself.

You might have heard Christians say that Jesus is "the Son of God", and that's true too. John calls him "the one and only Son, who came from the Father". But that doesn't take away from his "God-ness". The Bible speaks of God as Father, Son and Holy Spirit—all one, all distinct, all at the same time. So, says John, before he became human, the Son was "with God, and … was God", both at the same time (v 1).

Yet like Joshua Bell, Jesus traded his divine white tie and tails—his honour, glory and heavenly acclaim—for a life on the streets. Or literally, a stable. He lived the first 30 years of his life in poverty and anonymity. True greatness came in our midst, and most people walked past regardless.

The fact that "the Word became flesh" means that whatever you go through in life, *he gets you*. He understands you. Because he's been there himself—he experienced the full range of human emotions and experiences and heartaches.

Think of some of the hardest things you can go through in life.

Family arguments—Jesus has been there.

Mental anguish—Jesus has been there.

Life as a refugee on the run—Jesus has been there.

Bereavement of someone you dearly love—Jesus has been there.

Betrayal by one of your best friends—Jesus has been there.

National turmoil and political confusion—Jesus has been there.

Friends who fail you at your hour of need—Jesus has been there.

Being misinterpreted and unfairly represented—Jesus has been there.

Being ignored by the people you're trying to help—Jesus has been there.

Enduring physical pain—Jesus has been there.

Facing a fearful future—Jesus has been there.

Whatever it is, he gets it. He gets you. He became a human. God came in skin.

2. GOD CAME TO BE SEEN

"Ah..." you might be thinking, "It's all well and good claiming that God became a human... but I can't see him with my own eyes now. How can I know that any of this stuff really happened?"

Well, how do you know that Joshua Bell left the glories of the Symphony Hall to perform in squalor on the metro? Answer: because YouTube captured the moment for the rest of us.

Of course, YouTube hadn't been invented when God came to earth. (And that's probably just as well. Imagine 2000 years' worth of cat memes and prank videos.)

But they *did* have writing. So God ensured that everything important that Jesus said and did was captured by eyewitnesses and then written down.

Although Jesus grew up in a Middle Eastern backwater, when he set out as a travelling preacher and teacher at around age 30, it was all carried out in full view of the public: the religious and the irreligious, native Jewish people and occupying Romans, young and old, men and women... all saw and heard it.

Specifically, Jesus tasked his own followers, like John, with writing about it. John was one of Jesus' best friends, and his account of Jesus' life is one of the four historical biographies, or "Gospels", that we can find in the Bible. The others are Matthew, Mark and Luke. John and Matthew wrote from their own experience, and Mark seems to have written the eyewitness account of Jesus' close friend Peter. Luke was like an investigative journalist who interviewed eyewitnesses and collected the evidence after Jesus had died, risen and returned to heaven.

These Gospels were carefully written so that we can meet Jesus for ourselves as we read the pages of the Bible. So as we read John's Gospel, we can listen to Jesus' extraordinary teaching. We witness him befriend the outcasts of the society of that day—prostitutes and pariahs, foreigners and villains. We see him heal the deaf, the blind and the lame. And we watch him do what, quite frankly, only God could do. As John put it:

> *"We have seen his glory, the glory of the one and only Son."*

You see, when God showed up on the scene, he wasn't some 2-bit sideshow act that was hidden away in a corner. From his virgin birth onwards, Jesus was always on full display for all to see.

That is why it's so significant that the first witnesses of that first Christmas were the wise men from the east with their books and the working-class shepherds from the hills with their sheep. It's a pattern that continued as Jesus grew up: people from both ends of the social spectrum and from all over the ancient world recognised and worshipped Jesus as God on earth.

So if you've never really read the Bible as an adult, why not do that this Christmas? Dust down that old Bible from the shelf, or ask the person who gave you this booklet for a copy, or you can read it all online for free. Start with John's Gospel. Consider the eye-witness testimony with an open mind, and see what you make of Jesus. God came to be seen.

3. GOD CAME TO SAVE

> *"... the one and only Son, who came from the Father, full of grace and truth."*

Even if we're too old to believe in Santa, most of us still have a Santa-based approach to our presents. Deep down, we tend to think we deserve the gifts we're going to get on Christmas day. The good ones, that is—which is why we're so disappointed with diet books and pairs of socks. When we're kids we're told that that's the way that Santa works—he gives nice presents to the children who have earned their place on the nice list. Santa is only interested in the good little girls and good little boys.

And honestly, I'm not one of those.

Think about it. How far will you get into the new year before regret and frustration crop up again? Think of all the new year resolutions you'll make... and then break.

Or how far will most of us get into next year before we hurt our family or let down our friends yet again? If we even get that far... As friends and family come together at Christmas, many of us find that we're soon falling out over the most petty things.

Why is that? Why are we so quick to return kindness with selfishness?

I guess if we're all honest, we're far less nice than we like to admit. And the truth is that none of us are on the nice list when it comes to God.

It's easy to look quite good when we compare ourselves to other people. "Sure, I've said some things that were out of order and my self-control won't last," we think to ourselves, "But who cares? I'm better than *them*. I deserve a bit more from God than they do."

But stand alongside Jesus Christ for a minute. That's like a Grade 1 violinist standing next to Joshua Bell. We're going to be shown up for what we are.

But it gets even worse. After all, God is the King of the universe—our Maker, our Provider, the One who gives us life and breath and everything else. Our lives, including all the things we enjoy at this time of year, are a gift from him.

Yet we take the gift and say, "Clear off God". We hardly ever give him any thought—and when we do, it's only ever on our terms. We just take the gifts and ignore the giver like he's some Amazon delivery guy. We might nod politely as we sign for the package, but ultimately, we want to shut the door and get on with doing our own thing. And we only ever get in touch to complain when things don't go our way.

That's the reality—and it's something that God is rightly offended by. In fact, he's rightly angered by it.

But that is where the brilliant news of Christmas comes in. For in Jesus, God came to save. When "the Word became flesh", he came "full of grace and truth" (John 1 v 14).

"Grace" is the Bible's word for undeserved kindness—a totally free gift you could never earn. No good little girl or boy could qualify. It's a free gift for bad people.

"Truth" speaks of God keeping the promise he'd made to save people. For centuries before Jesus was born, God had spoken of sending a Rescuer for his people. He promised he'd come, and he *did* come. That's what the angel announced to the shepherds outside Bethlehem on that first Christmas night:

> *"Do not be afraid. I bring you good news that will cause great joy for all the people. Today in the town of David a Saviour has been born to you; he is the Messiah, the Lord." (Luke 2 v 10-11)*

If Jesus is a "Saviour", how does he save people? The answer is slightly surprising. John's Gospel goes on to explain that Jesus saves people by dying for them.

The Bethlehem baby at Christmas grew up to become the crucified Saviour at Easter. On the cross, because of his grace and truth, God treated Jesus as if he were you or me, so that he could treat you or me as if we were Jesus.

Here's how it works. I love lighting candles at Christmas. In fact, I think I might be a closet pyromaniac. But one of the most annoying things when you're trying to light a candle in the dark is when you open the match box and try to strike a match… only to find it's already been used. It doesn't work, because you can't burn the same thing twice. (Don't ask me what kind of person puts burnt matches back in the box. Probably the same person who puts empty wrappers back in the chocolate box.)

In a similar way, when Jesus Christ died on the cross, it was as if God burnt up all of his anger at the way I've treated him. Jesus experienced that judgment on my behalf and took it away.

You can't burn the same thing twice. So because God's righteous anger has been burned up, that means I can be forgiven, for everything in the past, for evermore in the future. I can be friends with God. The fire's been burnt. There's no more anger. I can know his smile. I can know his love. I can be friends with God.

And that's an offer that is open to you, too, this Christmas. The way we take up that offer is by trusting Jesus. That's not just a case of believing he exists, which there's so much evidence for (although that's part of it). It means trusting him—allowing him to bear your weight. It means asking him to take your mess and deal with it, so that you can be forgiven and live as a friend of God, forever. It means believing that Jesus died in your place and then rose to life, so that he can offer you new life.

WHAT NEXT?

Remember how *The Washington Post* described the Joshua Bell experiment as "a test of people's perceptions and priorities"? One good question to think about is: what's your perception and your priority in relation to Jesus Christ? Is he "just another" guy from history who's not really relevant, or is he something more?

The Christmas message is something that lots of people walk on past. But in this little booklet we've paused to listen to the music and pointed out who it is under the baseball cap. In the Christmas story, in Jesus, God became human, God was seen by witnesses, and God came to save us. So perhaps now you want to:

- **Stop and listen.** Maybe you like what you've heard, but you've got loads of questions. That's fair enough. You could ask the person who gave you this booklet or find a church where they teach the Bible. You can also find lots of answers to common questions online at **www.christianityexplored.org**. And the *best* way to keep listening to Jesus is to read the Bible. John's Gospel would be a good place to start.

- **Take a seat.** Maybe you're loving what you hear, and you want in on what Jesus offers. You're ready to sit down and enjoy his music. If that's you, you can pray these words to God right now:

  Dear God,

  Thank you for Christmas. Thank you that Jesus was willing to come and live as one of us. Thank you that whatever I'm facing this Christmas, he gets it.

  I'm sorry for the way that I've treated other people. I'm sorry for the way that I've treated you. I don't deserve anything from you.

  Thank you that Jesus came to offer me the free gift of forgiveness. I want him to take my sin and deal with it, so that I can live as your friend, forever.

Please help me to make Jesus a priority in my life, and show me more and more clearly who he is and how I can live his way.

Amen.

If you've prayed that and meant it, God has heard you and forgiven you. But that's only the start of the show! Now you can enjoy doing life with God: speaking to him in prayer, listening to him in the Bible and being part of his family, the church. And that will transform 25th December from "just another Christmas" into something really special.

We've all done Christmas before. So we know what to expect: the lights, the food, the tree, the traditions. But what if we've become so familiar with the trimmings that we've missed the main event?

Read this little booklet and discover three truths that can transform "just another Christmas" into something altogether more special.

"This could reset your perception of the wonder of Christmas."

RICO TICE

thegoodbook.com | .co.uk

Holidays / Christmas & Advent